The Art of Cosmic Connection: Exploring the Interconnected Universe and Energy Balance

By Gonzalo Estrada

THE ART OF COSMIC CONNECTION

First edition. March 12, 2024.

Copyright © 2024 Gonzalo Estrada.

ISBN: 979-8224133727

Written by Gonzalo Estrada.

Table of Contents

Contents

Chapter 1: The Awakening to Cosmic Connection

Chapter 1: The Awakening to Cosmic Connection

Introduction to the importance of cosmic connection in our lives and how to wake up to this reality to find energy balance.

In the vastness of the universe, everything is connected in a marvelous and mysterious way. The stars and the stars, the galaxies and the planets, everything intertwines in a cosmic dance that constantly envelops us. We are not mere spectators, but a fundamental part of this intricate universal fabric. In each of us, in the depths of our being, a spark of this cosmic connection throbs, waiting to be awakened.

In this chapter, we will delve into the depths of our existence to understand the importance of this connection and how we can awaken to it. Our goal is to find energy balance through a conscious link with the interconnected universe.

From time immemorial, different cultures have recognized the connection between human beings and the cosmos. The old masters knew that we are a small manifestation of a much larger whole. In their teachings, they conveyed the importance of understanding our relationship with the universe and how this can influence our daily lives.

Cosmic connection is much more than just a belief; it's a personal and profound experience. It is the awakening of a higher consciousness that allows us to understand that we are not alone or separate in this vast universe. We are a vital part of an interconnected network of energy and life.

As we awaken to the cosmic connection, we find an energy balance that transcends the ups and downs of life. We become aware of the forces and energies that surround us, and we learn to use them to our advantage. Through this awakening, we embrace a deeper understanding of ourselves and our purpose in this world.

How can we wake up to this reality and find energy balance? The answer lies in cultivating the connection with the universe. To do this, we must move away from the noise and distractions of modern life and seek moments of peace and reflection. It is in these moments of stillness that we can hear the subtle voice of the cosmos, which whispers its ancient wisdom to us.

Meditation and contemplation are powerful tools to open us up to this cosmic connection. By delving into ourselves and silencing our minds, we open up to the vastness of the universe. We feel how our energies are intertwined with the energies of the cosmos, and we experience a sense of unity and harmony.

Awakening to cosmic connection also involves opening up to the beauty that surrounds us. Every day, we witness amazing phenomena, from sunrise to the brightness of the stars at night. Observing nature in all its greatness reminds us of our connection to the universe and inspires us to live in harmony with it.

When we wake up to this cosmic connection, our perception of life is transformed. We become more aware of our own actions and how they impact the world around us. We understand that every thought, every word and every action have a resonance in the universe and in others.

Aware of this interconnection, we become agents of positive change in the world. We wake up to the power of our energy and how we can use it to create a significant impact in our lives and in the lives of others. We find the strength to overcome challenges and transcend our limitations, knowing that we are part of something much bigger.

In this first chapter, we have taken the first steps towards awakening the cosmic connection. We have explored the importance of this connection in our lives and how we can find energy balance through it.

However, this is only the tip of the iceberg of the mysteries and wonders that await.

In the next chapter, we will delve even deeper into the interconnected universe and discover ancient practices and teachings that will guide us on our path of cosmic connection. Get ready for a fascinating journey to the depths of your being and to understanding our place in this vast cosmos.

As we open ourselves to the cosmic connection, we immerse ourselves in a fascinating journey toward understanding our true essence and our place in the vast cosmos. As we delve deeper into this exploration, we discover that every aspect of our existence is intrinsically linked to the interconnected universe.

Over the centuries, sages and mystics have left us an invaluable legacy of practices and teachings that guide us to a deeper connection with the cosmos. These ancient traditions invite us to explore our inner being and to tune in to the cosmic energies that surround us.

One of the most powerful practices for cultivating this connection is meditation. By sitting in silence and quieting our mind, we open a direct channel with the universe. As we dive into the depth of our own consciousness, we become receptive to the subtle vibrations of the cosmos. In this state of stillness and harmony, we merge with universal energies and experience a sense of wholeness.

Meditation helps us to discover our true nature and to align our energies with the cosmic flow. Through regular practice, we become more aware of our energetic connection to everything around us. We realize that our actions and decisions have a direct impact on the balance of the universe and on the lives of those around us.

Another powerful practice for awakening our cosmic connection is the contemplation of beauty. As we open our senses to the wonders of the natural world, we connect with the deep harmony and perfection that exists in the universe. From a spectacular sunrise to the twinkling of the stars on a clear night, every manifestation of nature reminds us of our own uniqueness and our place in this cosmic vastness.

The cosmic connection also drives us to be aware of our actions and words in our interaction with others. We understand that we are interdependent beings, and every interaction we have can influence the well-being of others and the balance of the universe. By being aware of this, we cultivate an attitude of compassion and empathy towards others, knowing that we are all part of the same cosmic web.

As we awaken to our cosmic connection, we discover a deep sense of purpose in our lives. We become agents of positive change in the world, harnessing our energy and wisdom to improve our lives and the lives of others. We feel a deep resonance with the beauty and harmony of the universe and seek to live in tune with them.

This journey of cosmic connection is a personal and intimate journey. Each experience and each revelation bring us closer to understanding our true nature and our place in this vast interconnected cosmos. There are no shortcuts or magic formulas for this path, only a sincere and courageous openness to the truth that dwells within us.

As this first chapter concludes, I want to invite you to explore beyond these pages and to immerse yourself in the profound wisdom that ancient cultures and traditions have to offer. In the next few pages, we will discover age-old practices and teachings that will guide us on our path to cosmic connection and energy balance.

Get ready to embark on an amazing journey to the depths of your being and to understanding our place in this vast interconnected universe. May this awakening to cosmic connection led you to live in a state of harmony and wholeness, and may you find the energy balance you crave in every aspect of your existence.

The cosmic connection awaits us, ready to be discovered and experienced in all its glory. Go ahead, courageous explorer of the inner universe!

Chapter 2: The Nature of Universal Energy

The connection between us and the universe is much deeper than we normally perceive. As we explore the foundations of universal energy, we enter a fascinating world of cosmic interconnections and energy balance. How does this relate to our consciousness? What role does it play in our daily lives? In this chapter, we will take the first steps to understand the nature of universal energy and its influence on us as individuals.

From ancient times, various cultures have recognized the existence of a subtle energy that flows throughout the cosmos. The ancient Greeks called it ether, the Hindus called it prana, the Chinese called Qi. Although the names may vary, the essence is the same: we are all immersed in an ocean of energy that is constantly moving.

To understand universal energy, we must be aware that everything in the universe is composed of vibrating subatomic particles. These particles, in their essence, are pure energy. Quantum physics has revealed to us that even apparently solid matter is actually an energetic manifestation. As individual cells in the body of a vast organism, we are all connected to each other and to the universe through this energy.

Our consciousness, our ability to feel, think and experience, is also linked to this cosmic network of energy. When we attune our mind and heart to the universal flow, we open ourselves to the possibility of greater understanding and personal growth. It is through this conscious connection that we can explore and achieve energy balance in our lives.

However, it can be difficult to understand how this subtle energy impacts our daily experience. Often, we find ourselves stuck in routine and disconnected from our true energetic nature. But if we take a moment to look deeper, we can perceive its subtle effects on our moods, relationships, and overall well-being.

Universal energy flows through us and in turn, we are also capable of influencing it. Our thoughts, emotions, and intentions generate different energy frequencies that interact with the cosmos. Like the waves that propagate in a lake after a stone is thrown, our energies can expand and resonate in the universe, thus creating a ripple effect in our environment.

It's crucial to understand that our daily actions and choices have an impact not only on ourselves, but also on universal energy and those around us. Every day, we are immersed in a sea of energetic interactions, even though we are often unaware of it. Being able to consciously connect with this energy and use it in a positive way can transform both our personal reality and that of the world around us.

By exploring the foundations of universal energy, we embark on a path of self-discovery and expansion. We will be faced with profound questions about our own nature and our possibilities within the universe. Through understanding how our energies are intertwined with the whole, we can unlock infinite potential for spiritual growth and well-being.

So far, we have explored the first steps towards understanding universal energy and its connection with our consciousness. In the second part of this chapter, we'll delve even deeper into this fascinating topic and learn practices to strengthen our cosmic connection and balance our personal energies. Get ready for an exciting journey to explore our inner energy power. As we continue our exploration of universal energy and its connection with our consciousness, we embark on a fascinating journey toward a deeper understanding of our inner energy power. Through practices and techniques, we can strengthen our cosmic connection and balance our personal energies, allowing us to expand our horizons and achieve a higher state of well-being.

One of the most effective ways to strengthen our cosmic connection is through meditation. By channeling our attention to our inner world and focusing our mind on the energy flow that surrounds us, we can open up to a new dimension of consciousness. Meditation allows us to attune our personal vibration to that of the universe, establishing a harmony that fills us with peace and serenity.

During meditation, it's important to cultivate an attitude of openness and receptivity. By freeing our minds from limiting thoughts and judgments, we open ourselves to the infinite possibilities offered by the universe. Being present in the moment and allowing ourselves to flow with universal energy, allows us to experience a greater connection and understanding of everything that surrounds us.

Another powerful practice to strengthen our cosmic connection is creative visualization. By imagining vivid and vibrant images in our minds, we can give shape and direction to our energies. By visualizing ourselves in perfect balance and harmony, we can manifest that reality in our daily lives. Creative visualization allows us to explore and experience different possibilities and potentialities, thus creating a bridge between our desires and the universal energy that surrounds us.

It's important to remember that our daily choices and actions have a direct impact on our personal energy and on the universal energy flow. Therefore, it is essential to practice self-observation and self-awareness. By paying attention to our thoughts, emotions, and actions, we can identify patterns that take us away from energy balance and take steps to correct them.

In addition, the regular practice of gratitude and generosity allows us to open our hearts and expand our energy to others. By recognizing and valuing the blessings we receive in our lives and by sharing our blessings with others, we create a dynamic of positive energy exchange that nourishes us all. Gratitude and generosity allow us to flow into the energy of abundance and to nourish our relationships with love and compassion.

On this journey toward exploring our inner energy, we must also remember that we are interconnected beings in a vast and dynamic universe. Our actions and choices not only affect ourselves, but they also impact collective energy. Therefore, it is essential to honor and respect the energy of others, recognizing that we are all part of the same cosmic web.

In short, universal energy is a vital force that flows throughout the cosmos, connecting us to the universe and to each other. Our consciousness is intrinsically linked to this cosmic web of energy, and we can strengthen our cosmic connection through practices such as meditation, creative visualization, and the cultivation of gratitude and generosity. By being aware of our daily choices and actions, we can balance our personal energies and contribute positively to the universal energy flow. On this journey of self-discovery and expansion, we open up to our infinite potential for spiritual growth and well-being.

Chapter 3: The Power of Intuition

A journey towards understanding intuition as a powerful guide to connecting with the cosmos and achieving energy balance.

The power of intuition is something that has fascinated mankind since time immemorial. Throughout history, we have felt that inner voice that whispers, guides us and connects us to something greater than ourselves. Intuition is like a beacon in the dark, a heavenly compass that shows us the way when our rational minds fall short.

On our journey to understanding intuition, we must set aside the barriers of conventional thinking and open our minds to new possibilities. Intuition does not follow the rules of logic and reason, but is nourished by ancient wisdom and deep connection with the cosmos.

Intuition is that subtle feeling that alerts us when something isn't right, or drives us to make decisions that can change our lives. This is not something random or casual, but a powerful and authentic force that resides within us and connects us to the interconnected universe.

To understand intuition, we must learn to listen to and trust it. Often, our rational minds try to discredit it, calling it an illusion or coincidence. However, if we open up to it and give it the space it deserves, we will discover its true power.

Intuition cannot be forced or controlled. It's like that gentle breeze that caresses our face on a summer day; we can feel its presence, but we can't catch it or control its direction. It's a fluid and mysterious phenomenon that we must learn to appreciate and respect.

Connecting with intuition is an intimate and personal process. It requires a greater level of awareness and presence in our being. Often, we are so engrossed in the maelstrom of our daily lives that we disconnect from our inner voice. But if we find moments of calm and silence, we can hear that whispering voice that guides us and gives us answers.

Intuition is also closely related to energy balance. When we are in harmony with our inner being and with the cosmos, our intuition becomes clearer and stronger. Conversely, when we find ourselves out of balance and disconnected, our intuition weakens and we lose that sense of guidance and purpose.

It's important to learn to discern between genuine intuition and the noises in our minds. Sometimes, our expectations, fears, and desires can cloud our true intuition. We must learn to listen with an open heart and mind, without prejudice or judgment.

When we trust our intuition and let ourselves be guided by it, we begin to experience a deeper connection with the cosmos. We become co-creators of our reality and open ourselves to a world of infinite possibilities. Intuition is a powerful tool that allows us to move beyond the limits of our rational mind and explore the vast interconnected universe.

In the second half of this chapter, we'll explore how we can cultivate and strengthen our intuition. We will learn practices that will help us to tune in to our inner wisdom and to access cosmic guidance in our daily lives. But before we enter this part of the journey, let's leave the conclusion of this chapter suspended and allow the seed of intuition to germinate in our minds, leaving room for the wonder and surprise that the next part of this exploration will bring. In this second part of our journey to the power of intuition, we will immerse ourselves in practices and techniques that will help us cultivate and strengthen our connection with our inner wisdom and cosmic guidance. Through these tools, we will learn to attune to our intuition in our daily lives.

One of the most effective ways to strengthen our intuition is to practice meditation. Meditation allows us to calm our minds and make room to listen to our inner voice. By taking a few minutes a day to sit in silence and direct our attention to our breathing, we can train our mind to be receptive to intuitive messages. Over time, we'll notice how our intuition becomes clearer and more accurate.

Another useful practice to strengthen our intuition is to keep a dream diary. Our dreams are a gateway to our subconscious and can reveal valuable intuitive messages. By keeping a journal and writing down our dreams as soon as we wake up, we can begin to recognize patterns and symbols that help us interpret the messages our subconscious sends us. By paying attention to and reflecting on our dreams, we will be nourishing and strengthening our intuition.

In addition to meditation and dream journaling, it's important to cultivate trust in our intuition. Often, we doubt our hunches and ignore them when making important decisions in our lives. However, trusting our intuition allows us to align our steps with the cosmic order and find an energetic balance in our actions. By allowing us to be guided by our intuition and to make decisions based on it, we open the doors to new possibilities and synchronicities in our lives.

Another technique we can use to strengthen our intuition is visualization. By closing our eyes and imagining specific situations and scenarios, we activate our imagination and connect with our intuition. We can visualize a goal or decision and see how our intuition guides us to the next step to take. Visualization allows us to access our inner wisdom and unlock answers in a powerful and creative way.

Finally, it's important to remember that our journey toward understanding intuition is unique and personal. Each of us has our own path to explore and develop this connection with the cosmos. As we navigate the waters of our intuition, it's essential to practice patience and self-compassion. There is no final destination, but rather a continuous blossoming of our intuitive power as we delve into our own exploration.

As this chapter concludes, we are left with the gift of intuition as a reliable compass on our journey through the cosmos. By trusting our inner wisdom and attuning to our cosmic connection, we will discover an energy balance and guidance that transcend the limitations of our rational mind.

In the next chapter, we will continue our journey of exploration and immerse ourselves in the mystery and wonder of the interconnected universe. But for now, let the seed of intuition continue to grow inside us and remember that we are constantly evolving cosmic beings, always connected to the energy balance of the vast universe in which we inhabit.

Let us move forward, with open hearts and curious minds, in search of a deeper connection with ourselves and the cosmos that surrounds us.

Chapter 4: Healing Through Energy Connections

In the vast interconnected universe in which we live, there is a constant flow of energies that surrounds and envelops us. These energies, both physical and emotional, have a profound impact on our overall well-being and balance. In this chapter, we'll explore the ways in which cosmic connection can facilitate emotional and physical healing, giving us a powerful tool to restore and balance our being.

As we embark on the journey of healing through energy connections, it is essential to understand that we are part of a larger cosmic fabric. Everything in the universe is interconnected, from the stars that shine high in the sky to the atoms that make up our own bodies. This interconnection allows us to access a constant flow of healing energies that we can harness for our own benefit.

One of the most powerful ways to connect to this energy flow is through mindfulness and meditation. By cultivating the ability to center our mind and attune to the present, we can open ourselves to receiving healing energies. Mindfulness allows us to be aware of our emotions and physical sensations, and by doing so, we can begin to heal those aspects of our being that need attention.

Cosmic connection can also facilitate emotional healing by providing a sense of belonging and purpose. By recognizing that we are part of something bigger and that our experiences and sufferings are interconnected with those of other human beings, we can find comfort and understanding in the midst of adversity. In this sense, the cosmic connection invites us not to feel alone in our struggles, but to find strength and support in the interconnected web of existence.

In addition to mindfulness and the search for emotional connections, cosmic connection can also facilitate physical healing. As we explore and understand the energy patterns that flow through our body, we can use this information to promote balance and healing. Through practices such as acupuncture, reflexology and Reiki, we can channel and direct universal energy to specific areas of our body that need healing.

Cosmic connection invites us to expand our vision of life and to recognize that we are part of a greater whole. In doing so, we open the doors to new perspectives and possibilities for healing. This holistic approach considers that our emotions, thoughts and physical bodies are intrinsically connected and that balance and harmony can only be achieved by addressing every aspect of our existence.

As we delve deeper into the exploration of cosmic energy connections and their role in healing, we are faced with a range of opportunities to restore our well-being. In the second half of this chapter, we will explore specific practices and techniques that help us to strengthen our connection to the cosmic energy flow and to use it for emotional and physical healing in our everyday lives.

The connection with the universe is an infinite and exciting journey that invites us to discover and explore our own healing capacities. Allow yourself to immerse yourself in this experience and prepare your mind and heart for the surprises and revelations that the next chapter has in store for you. For now, let the idea of a cosmic connection envelop you and feel the universal energy flowing through you, preparing you for a profound and healing transformation.

It will continue... Cosmic energy connections provide us with a unique opportunity for healing and transformation. As we delve deeper into this journey, we discover practices and techniques that help us strengthen our connection to the cosmic energy flow and use it to heal our daily lives.

One of these powerful practices is conscious breathing. Through mindfulness in our breathing, we can calm our mind and connect to the universal rhythm of the universe. With each inhalation, we receive vital energy and with each exhalation, we release any emotional tension or discomfort. Conscious breathing allows us to be aware of our bodies and emotions, and it gives us a tool to release what no longer serves us and receive renewed energy.

Another technique that can facilitate cosmic connection and healing is visualization. By closing our eyes and visualizing that we are surrounded by a cosmic light, we can invoke and receive healing energies. Imagine this light flowing through each of your cells, restoring and balancing your entire being. By visualizing this connection, we open up to the wisdom and power of the universe, allowing its healing energies to guide us in our healing process.

In addition to conscious breathing and visualization, practicing gratitude can also have a profound impact on our emotional and physical well-being. By focusing on the blessings and positive experiences in our lives, we raise our energy vibration and open ourselves up to receiving even more blessings. Gratitude helps us expand our consciousness and connect to the love and abundance of the universe, contributing to our physical and emotional healing.

On our healing journey through cosmic energy connections, it's also important to remember that we are multidimensional beings. We are not only connected to the energy flow of the universe, but also to higher aspects of our own consciousness. By cultivating the connection with our higher self, we access greater wisdom and deeper inner guidance. Through meditation and contemplation, we can open up to this connection and receive guidance in our healing process.

As we move forward in our exploration of cosmic energy connections and their role in healing, we realize that healing is an ongoing journey. There is no final destination, but rather a path of constant growth and transformation. Every day, we have the opportunity to connect with the energy flow of the universe and use it to heal and balance our being.

At the end of this chapter, I invite you to reflect on how you can integrate these practices and techniques into your daily life. Allow yourself to explore and experiment with cosmic energy connections, and trust that you have the power to heal and transform your life. Remember that you are part of a greater whole and that you have access to a constant flow of healing energies.

Feel the cosmic connection around you and within you, and allow yourself to be guided by its transformative power. Trust that you are on the right path and prepare for a profound and healing transformation.

Thank you for joining me on this journey of exploration and healing through cosmic energy connections. May these words inspire you to continue your own journey of growth and transformation, and may you find the healing you seek in connection with the interconnected universe and energy balance.

Chapter 5: The Influence of Relationships on Energy Balance

Our personal relationships are an integral part of our lives. Through them, we establish deep connections with others, and these interactions can have a significant impact on our state of energy balance. Every relationship we cultivate, whether with family, friends, coworkers or romantic partners, influences our level of cosmic connection and, therefore, our inner harmony.

When we interact with other people, we exchange energies. The energy we transmit and receive can be positive or negative, and this directly affects our inner balance. For example, a conflicting or toxic relationship can drain our vital energy, while a harmonious and loving relationship can nourish us and raise our vibration.

It is essential to become aware of how our personal relationships affect us. It is necessary to examine both the relationships that provide us with an enriching experience and those that may be unbalancing our energy well-being. Often, we don't realize the influence these relationships have on us, simply because we've gotten used to them or because we're afraid to face reality.

To maintain a healthy energy balance in our relationships, it's essential to set clear, healthy boundaries. We must learn to say "no" when necessary, as carrying more commitments than we can handle can exhaust us physically and emotionally. It's important to remember that we can't provide our support and unconditional love if we're not taking care of our own energy.

In addition, it's critical to prioritize our emotional needs in our relationships. Often, we find ourselves in situations where we sacrifice ourselves to meet the needs of others, neglecting our own emotions in the process. This can lead to an energy imbalance in our cosmic connection and negatively affect our ability to maintain healthy relationships.

It's also important to foster relationships based on authenticity and sincerity. When we are vulnerable and sincere with others, we establish a deeper level of connection and strengthen the energy balance in our interaction. By letting go of masks and emotional barriers, we create a safe space where both parties can grow and evolve together.

As we explore how personal relationships affect our level of cosmic connection, it's essential to remember that every relationship is a mirror of ourselves. The people we attract into our lives reflect both our strengths and our areas of growth. Often, the most difficult lessons in our interactions are meant to help us evolve and find greater energy balance.

In short, our personal relationships have a profound impact on our level of cosmic connection and energy balance. We need to become aware of how each relationship affects us and set healthy boundaries to maintain our own energy. By prioritizing our emotional needs, fostering authentic relationships, and recognizing the lessons that relationships provide, we can cultivate a deeper cosmic connection and maintain energy balance in our lives.

It's critical to remember that every relationship we cultivate is a mirror of ourselves, which means that our interactions are a reflection of our inner strengths and weaknesses. Often, the people we attract into our lives are a reminder of the lessons we must learn and the areas in which we must grow to find greater energy balance.

To maintain a healthy balance in our relationships, it's also vital to practice forgiveness and compassion. No one is perfect, and we all make mistakes in our personal interactions. However, holding on to resentments and grudges only feeds negativity and prevents us from finding inner peace. Learning to forgive and let go of the past allows us to release negative energies and make room for healing and growth.

In addition, it's crucial to establish a sense of gratitude in our relationships. Often, we focus on what we lack or on the frustrations we experience with others. However, by focusing on what we appreciate and value in the people around us, we nurture energy balance in our interactions. Expressing gratitude and recognition to those around us fosters positive dynamics and strengthens our cosmic connection.

On the path to energy balance in our relationships, we must also remember the importance of clear and open communication. Often, misunderstandings and assumptions are the source of conflicts and imbalances in our personal connections. Taking the time to express our needs, concerns, and expectations allows us to set healthy boundaries and better understand others.

It's also essential to establish quality moments in our relationships. Modern life can be hectic and busy, which can result in a lack of time and attention to those we love. However, setting aside time to be together, to talk and to enjoy shared experiences strengthens the bond and nourishes the cosmic connection.

In addition, we must be willing to commit and adapt in our relationships. Energy balance is not about always being right, but about allowing a harmonious flow of energy between us and others. Being flexible and open to new perspectives and ways of doing things encourages balanced and enriching interaction.

Ultimately, it's important to remember that we are individual beings who deserve love and respect, as do those with whom we relate. Maintaining energy balance in our relationships involves honoring and nourishing our own energy, setting limits, and practicing self-care. We can't provide support and unconditional love if we're not taking care of ourselves.

In conclusion, our personal relationships have a significant impact on our level of cosmic connection and energy balance. Through awareness, setting healthy boundaries, gratitude, clear communication, quality time together, flexibility, and self-care, we can maintain a healthy balance in our personal connections. As we continue to explore the influences of relationships on energy balance, let us remember that love, empathy, and compassion are fundamental to cultivating a deeper and more meaningful cosmic connection. On this journey, it's important to be kind to both others and to ourselves, remembering that we are all constantly growing and learning.

Chapter 6: Energy Cycles: Moon, Sun, and More

Exploring the energy cycles of the moon, the sun and other cosmic phenomena that affect our energy and how to harness them to our advantage.

The connection between us and the cosmos is undeniable. Even if we can't see it at first glance, the energy cycles of the moon, the sun and other cosmic phenomena influence our lives in subtle but significant ways. In this chapter, we'll dive deep into the exploration of these cosmic cycles and how we can harness them to our advantage.

Let's start with the moon, a heavenly body that has captivated humanity throughout history. Its influence on ocean tides is already widely known, but did you know that it also affects our energy? The moon goes through different phases, from the new moon to the full moon, and each of these phases has its own unique energy.

During the new moon, a period of darkness, the perfect opportunity to reflect and set intentions for the future presents itself. It is a time of renewal and sowing the seeds of our desires. As the moon grows, so do our energies and our projects. It's a good time to take action and give life to our goals.

The full moon, on the other hand, shines in all its splendor and fills us with expansive energy. It's a time of clarity and fullness, where our emotions are on the surface. Take this time to recognize your achievements and celebrate them. However, we must also remember that the full moon can bring with it an intensification of our emotions, so it is important to maintain balance and take care of our energy.

But the energy cycle isn't just limited to the moon. The sun, the source of life and energy, also plays a fundamental role in our cosmic connection. Every day, the sun gives us its light and warmth, providing vital energy to nourish our body and soul. The sunrise marks the beginning of a new cycle, while the sunset invites us to reflect on the day that has just passed.

In addition to the moon and the sun, there are other cosmic phenomena that influence our energy. From planetary movements to stellar cycles, each of them has its own impact on our daily lives. These cosmic events can be an opportunity to tune in to the energies of the universe and align our intentions with the greater forces that surround us.

It's important to remember that while these cosmic cycles can influence our energy, we also have the ability to influence them. We are cosmic beings in an interconnected universe, and our energy is intertwined with that of everything around us. By being aware of these energy cycles, we can use them to our advantage and enhance our intentions.

In the second part of this chapter, we'll explore some practices and techniques for harnessing these energy cycles to our advantage. From moonlight rituals to sun-guided meditations, we'll discover how we can attune to the cosmos and balance our energies. But that, dear readers, will be a journey that you will continue in the next installment.

So, for now, I invite you to immerse yourself in the magic of these energy cycles and to reflect on their influence on our lives. Let the cosmic connection inspire you to explore new dimensions of your being and to discover how to harness these forces to your advantage. Let's get ready for what's to come, because the universe always has something in store for those willing to listen to its energetic whispers. Continuation:

In our quest for energy balance, it's important to understand that cosmic cycles aren't just limited to the moon and the sun. There are other phenomena that also influence our energy and connect us to the universe in a profound way.

One of them is the movement of the planets. Each of them has their own energy and personality, and their influence on our lives can be subtle but significant. For example, Mercury, the planet of communication and mind, urges us to reflect and to be clear in our words. Venus, the planet of love and beauty, inspires us to take care of ourselves and to cultivate harmonious relationships. Mars, the planet of action and passion, impels us to make courageous decisions and to pursue our dreams with determination.

In addition to planets, stellar cycles also have their power. The stars guide us in the dark of the night and remind us that we are part of something bigger. Observing the constellations and immersing yourself in the magic of the starry sky can help us find direction, inspiration and serenity in the midst of our daily challenges.

To make the most of these cosmic cycles, it is necessary to cultivate a conscious connection with them. There are several practices and techniques that we can incorporate into our daily routine to tune in to the energy of the universe and use it to our advantage.

One of the most powerful ways to do this is through meditation. Taking time each day to sit in silence, breathe deeply, and connect with cosmic energy can help us find balance and align our intentions with the greater forces around us. We can visualize how the sun fills us with light and energy, how the moon guides us in our reflections or how the stars provide us with their wisdom and constancy.

Another powerful practice is the observation of natural cycles. Taking a moment to appreciate the beauty of a sunrise or sunset, to admire the moon in all its phases or to contemplate the starry sky connects us to the greatness of the cosmos and invites us to be an active part of it. We can record our observations in a cosmic diary and reflect on how we feel in each phase of the moon, at each moment of the day or in the presence of a certain star.

In addition to these practices, we can also take advantage of specific rituals for each energy cycle. For example, during the full moon, we can perform a liberation ritual, writing on paper what we want to release and then burning it, letting the fire transform and release that energy. During the new moon, we can create a list of intentions and visualize how they are manifested in our lives as the moon grows.

By exploring these energy cycles and using them to our advantage, we open up to a deeper and more meaningful experience of our cosmic connection. We become co-creators of the universe, conscious beings capable of attuning to the highest energies and of manifesting our deepest desires.

To conclude this chapter, I want to remind you that cosmic connection is an inexhaustible resource. As you continue to explore energy cycles and discover new ways to harness them, you'll be amazed at the wisdom and guidance the universe has in store for you.

So, I invite you to continue exploring, to continue to tune in to the energy of the cosmos and to allow its energetic whispers to guide you on your path. You are part of something bigger, dear reader, and by recognizing it, you can find a new dimension of power and gratitude in your life.

May each cosmic cycle inspire you to live with passion and purpose, and may every connection you make with the universe bring you closer to achieving the balance and wholeness you deserve.

Chapter 7: The Importance of Meditation and Introspection

Cosmic connection and energy balance are fundamental to achieving a full and harmonious life. On our journey of exploring the interconnected universe, we find ourselves with the need to strengthen this connection and maintain an appropriate energy balance. To this end, meditation and introspection are presented as essential tools that allow us to delve into our own being, to better understand ourselves and to find the inner peace we need.

Meditation has been practiced since ancient times by different cultures and traditions, and its importance has been maintained over time. It is a practice that invites us to calm our minds and direct our attention to the present, allowing us to free ourselves from the worries of the past and the expectations of the future. By focusing on the present moment, we immerse ourselves in the experience of our inner being and connect with the cosmic energy that surrounds us.

Through meditation, we can observe our thoughts, emotions, and sensations objectively, without judging or clinging to them. This mindfulness helps us recognize our thinking patterns, identify the causes of our emotions, and better understand our reactions to different situations. By knowing ourselves more deeply, we can make decisions that are more conscious and aligned with our true essence.

Introspection, on the other hand, is the tool that allows us to delve into our own essence and explore the deepest layers of our being. Through reflection and self-analysis, we approach our motivations, beliefs and values. Taking the time to explore our inner world allows us to recognize our most authentic wants and needs, and gives us the opportunity to align our lives with them.

Meditation and introspection, used together, offer us a deep connection with the universe and an energy balance that helps us to face the challenges of everyday life. By exploring our inner being, we open ourselves to the possibility of transforming and evolving into a more conscious and fulfilling version of ourselves.

Meditation helps us to calm our minds and find clarity amidst the constant flow of thoughts that surround us. Through regular practice, we develop the ability to observe our thoughts and emotions without being trapped by them. This ability allows us to distance ourselves from mental turmoil and to open up to a broader vision of reality.

On the other hand, introspection gives us the opportunity to examine our motivations and actions, and to assess whether we are living according to our deepest values. By reflecting on our experiences and drawing lessons from them, we can grow and improve as people. Introspection invites us to question ourselves and explore our own inner world, in search of answers and wisdom.

Cosmic connection and energy balance are essential to our existence in this vast interconnected universe. Meditation and introspection provide us with the tools necessary to strengthen this connection and maintain that balance. By exploring our inner being, we deepen our understanding and experience greater wholeness in our lives.

It is in moments of silence and reflection that we find answers to our deepest questions and discover the fundamental truths that connect us to the universe. In the second part of this chapter, we'll further explore meditative practices and introspection, delving into how we can use them to cultivate that cosmic connection and maintain energy balance in our daily lives. Together, we will discover the secrets hidden in our own being and in the vast cosmos. The second half of this chapter will take us to further explore the practices of meditation and introspection, delving into how we can use them to cultivate that cosmic connection and maintain energy balance in our daily lives. Through these tools, men and women will find a greater sense of inner peace and greater clarity in our paths.

Meditation gives us a space to immerse ourselves and connect with our deepest essence. As we continue to practice meditation, we become more aware of our emotions and thoughts, and we develop the ability to observe them without judging or clinging to them. This attitude of acceptance allows us to free ourselves from the emotional and mental burdens that prevent us from achieving inner peace.

As we gain experience in meditation, we can also experience moments of deep cosmic connection. Through constant practice, our senses sharpen and our perception expands. We can feel the energy flowing around us and recognize our interconnection with the universe. This cosmic connection invites us to live a life more aligned with the natural flow of energy and allows us to find greater harmony in our thoughts, emotions and actions.

Introspection, on the other hand, gives us the opportunity to explore our inner world and discover our true nature. By reflecting on our experiences and questioning ourselves, we can identify patterns of thinking and behavior that take us away from energy balance. Through self-analysis, we find the answers and solutions that help us to stay in harmony with ourselves and with the universe.

It's important to note that both meditation and introspection require time and dedication. They are not practices that we can master overnight, but they require patience and perseverance. However, the benefits we can derive from them are immense.

By strengthening our cosmic connection and maintaining an appropriate energy balance, we open ourselves to a life full of meaningful opportunities and experiences. We become conscious observers of our own being and of the universe around us. By finding inner peace and harmony, we become co-creators of our lives, manifesting our most authentic desires and purpose.

In short, meditation and introspection invite us to immerse ourselves in our own being, to explore our connection with the universe and to discover our true essence. Through these practices, men and women find the opportunity to achieve an adequate energy balance and live a full and harmonious life.

In moments of silence and reflection, we find the answers to our deepest questions and discover the fundamental truths that connect us to the vast cosmos. By continuing to cultivate these practices in our daily lives, we embrace our personal power and become conscious, connected beings.

This is how we conclude this chapter, having explored the importance of meditation and introspection as essential tools for cultivating a cosmic connection and maintaining an energetic balance. In the next chapter, we will continue our journey through the interconnected universe and explore new practices and concepts that are fundamental to our personal growth and development.

Chapter 8: The Wisdom of Ancient Traditions

Exploring the teachings of ancient traditions in relation to cosmic connection and how we can apply them to our current lives.

Cosmic connection is a topic that has fascinated humanity since time immemorial. Throughout history, different cultures have developed wisdom and knowledge about this connection and how we can relate to the interconnected universe that surrounds us. In this chapter, we will explore the teachings of ancient traditions in relation to this cosmic connection and how we can apply them to our current lives.

Ancient traditions have recognized the importance of connecting with the cosmos for thousands of years. Cultures such as the ancient Egyptians, Mayans, Hindus and Aboriginal Australians have left behind a legacy of wisdom that invites us to explore our relationship with the universe in a deeper way.

One of the key teachings of these traditions is the notion that we are an integral part of the cosmos. Not only are we connected to each other as human beings, but we are also connected to everything around us, including the stars, planets and the entire universe. This connection is not only physical, but also spiritual and energetic.

In ancient Egyptian culture, for example, gods were believed to be present in every aspect of nature. Each element had its own spirit and was connected to the others. This holistic view of the cosmos led them to develop complex religious systems and spiritual practices that sought to harmonize the connection between human beings and the universe.

Similarly, the ancient traditions of the Mayans and Hindus also recognized the importance of cosmic connection. The Mayans built elaborate astronomical observatories and precise calendars that reflected their understanding of the relationship between the stars and human beings. For their part, Hindus developed the philosophical system of yoga that seeks to unite mind, body and spirit to achieve harmony and connection with the cosmos.

These ancient teachings also invite us to reflect on how we can apply this wisdom in our daily lives. In an increasingly interconnected world, we often feel disconnected from ourselves and from others. Technology and the speed of the modern world have taken us away from our essential connection to the cosmos.

However, ancient traditions offer us tools and practices to reconnect with our true cosmic essence. Meditation, for example, is a practice that allows us to calm our minds and find a space of inner stillness, allowing us to experience our connection with the universe on a deeper level.

In the same way, the connection with nature is essential to reestablish our cosmic connection. When we take the time to admire a sunrise, stroll through a forest, or get lost in the sound of ocean waves, we open our hearts to the greatness of the universe and remember our connection to it.

In short, the teachings of ancient traditions invite us to become aware of our cosmic connection and to explore how we can apply this wisdom to our current lives. As we deepen our understanding of the connection between the universe and ourselves, we open up to a greater sense of harmony and energy balance. In the second part of this chapter, we will explore specific practices and rituals that will help us strengthen this cosmic connection and integrate it into our daily lives. In the second part of this chapter, we will continue our exploration of the teachings of ancient traditions in relation to cosmic connection and how we can apply them to our current lives. Now, we will delve into specific practices and rituals that will help us to strengthen this cosmic connection and to integrate it into our daily lives.

One of the most powerful practices for cultivating cosmic connection is the contemplation of starry skies. For thousands of years, ancient cultures have observed and studied stars as a way of understanding their place in the cosmos. Taking the time to go outside on a clear night and observe the night sky can be a profoundly transformative experience. By admiring the constellations and planets, we can feel our smallness compared to the vastness of the universe and, at the same time, recognize our intimate connection with it.

Another practice that ancient traditions teach us is the fire ceremony. Fire has been considered sacred in many cultures and has been used to communicate with the gods and to purify the spirit. Lighting a campfire or candle and dedicating a moment of reflection and gratitude to the fire can help us connect with cosmic energy. Watching the dancing flames and feeling the warmth that emanates from them can remind us of the life force that flows through us and how we are in harmony with the inner fire of the universe.

In addition, ancient traditions also invite us to use tools such as crystals and gemstones to strengthen our cosmic connection. These objects contain unique energies and are believed to help us balance and harmonize our own energies. For example, transparent quartz is considered an energy amplifier and can help us tune in to cosmic energy, while amethyst is associated with spiritual connection and intuition. Carrying these stones with us or placing them in our home or workplace can be an effective way to remind us of our connection to the universe.

In addition, the connection with the body is also essential to strengthen our cosmic connection. Ancient traditions teach us that the body is a sacred temple and that we have a responsibility to care for and nourish it properly. Practicing mindful eating, making time for physical exercise and rest, and paying attention to our emotional and spiritual needs are some ways to honor our bodies and, in turn, cultivate a deeper connection with the cosmos.

Finally, music and art can also be powerful tools for exploring our cosmic connection. Throughout history, ancient cultures have used music and dance as means of communicating with the divine. Playing a musical instrument, singing or dancing allows us to express our deepest essence and connect with the creative energy of the universe. In the same way, art in all its forms allows us to express our unique vision of the world and to capture the beauty and mystery of the cosmos.

In conclusion, the teachings of ancient traditions offer us a treasure trove of practices and rituals to strengthen our cosmic connection and live in harmony with the universe. By contemplating starry skies, performing fire ceremonies, using crystals and gemstones, caring for our bodies and exploring music and art, we open the doors to a deeper experience of connection and energy balance. In our daily lives, we can find moments to practice these activities and thus remember our true cosmic nature. The wisdom of ancient traditions guides us to a fuller and more connected life in this interconnected universe.

Chapter 9: The Balance Between Giving and Receiving

Our interactions with other human beings and with the universe in general are in constant flux of giving and receiving energy. This cosmic dance of interconnection is essential for our well-being and emotional balance. In our daily encounters, both with close friends and with strangers, our energies intertwine and intertwine, creating an interconnected universe of mutual influences.

It is important to reflect on the importance of maintaining a balance in our energetic interactions, both in giving and in receiving. The balance between these two fundamental poles allows us to find harmony and peace in our relationships with others and with the world around us.

When we become energetically unbalanced, whether we are focused solely on giving or receiving, we lose our connection with the flow of the universe. Sometimes, we can find ourselves stuck in a cycle of giving without receiving, exhausting our own energy reserves and leaving us empty. On the other hand, we can also fall into the trap of only receiving without giving, which can generate a feeling of selfishness and lack of connection with others.

The first step toward balance is to be aware of our own needs and the needs of others. It's important to recognize that we are all interdependent beings, in need of emotional support and nourishment. By realizing this, we can begin to cultivate a healthy balance between giving and receiving.

When we give, we can do so from a place of authentic and selfless generosity. Offering a friendly smile, a helping hand, or simply listening intently can be powerful gestures of giving positive energy to others. However, it's also essential to set healthy limits and to ensure that we don't exhaust our own reserves. Being able to say "no" when necessary and taking care of our own health and well-being allows us to be more whole and aware beings.

Similarly, receiving is a gift in itself. By opening ourselves to accepting support from others, we provide ourselves with the opportunity to be emotionally nourished and to allow others to share their love and care with us. Accepting and receiving without guilt or shame is an act of self-love and allows us to strengthen our connections with others.

The key to maintaining balance in our energetic interactions lies in awareness and intention. Being aware of our own needs and limits, as well as the needs and limits of others, helps us to establish a healthy dynamic in our relationships.

In short, the balance between giving and receiving is essential for our energetic and emotional health. Maintaining full awareness and loving intention allows us to find harmony in our daily interactions. In the next chapter, we'll explore how we can cultivate and strengthen this balance in our lives.

In this second part of the chapter, we will delve into some practical strategies to cultivate and strengthen the balance between giving and receiving in our lives.

One of the most powerful tools we can use is the practice of gratitude. By being aware and thankful for the good things we receive on a daily basis, we open ourselves to a constant flow of positive energy. When we are attuned to this flow of thankfulness, we become magnets of more blessings and abundance. Gratitude allows us to recognize the generosity of others and to value the gifts they offer us, whether big or small.

Another important strategy is regular self-reflection. Taking the time to evaluate our interactions with others allows us to detect any energy imbalance and correct it before it becomes a bigger problem. Ask yourself: Am I giving more than I am receiving? Am I constantly exhausting myself without getting the care and support I need? Am I receiving without offering anything in return? These questions help us stay aware of our actions and provide us with an opportunity to adjust our approach if necessary.

In addition, it's essential to set clear boundaries in our relationships. Sometimes, we may feel pressured to give more than we feel comfortable or able to provide. Learning to say "no" and set healthy boundaries is an act of self-love and empowerment. We shouldn't feel guilty for putting our health and well-being first. By setting clear boundaries, we protect ourselves from exhausting our energy reserves and we also help to keep the dynamics balanced in our relationships.

Another aspect to consider is the importance of taking care of our own health and well-being. When we're out of balance energetically, it can be difficult to find satisfaction and joy in our interactions. Making time for self-care, seeking activities that nourish us emotionally and physically, and surrounding ourselves with people who support and inspire us can be effective ways to recharge our energies and maintain balance.

Finally, let's remember that giving and receiving is not only limited to our interactions with others, but it also includes our relationship with ourselves and the universe. Taking time to connect with our inner being, seeking moments of silence and meditation, and being open to receiving the answers and guidance that the universe offers us are fundamental aspects on our path to inner balance.

In conclusion, the balance between giving and receiving is an ongoing process that requires awareness, intention, and practice. By staying aware of our actions and needs, setting healthy limits, and taking care of our own health and well-being, we can cultivate an energy balance that allows us to find harmony and peace in our relationships with others and with the universe. Remember, giving and receiving are two sides of the same coin, and by honoring both poles, we open ourselves to a constant flow of love and positive energy in our lives.

Continue to explore and practice these strategies for balance in your own life, and you'll discover how this cosmic connection will bring you to a state of greater wholeness and fulfillment.

Chapter 10: The Power of Creative Visualization

Exploring how creative visualization can help us to manifest our intentions and strengthen our cosmic connection.

Creative visualization, a powerful and transformative tool, invites us to enter a world of infinite possibilities and to co-create our reality. Through visualization, we can form vivid and clear mental images of what we want to manifest in our lives. By strengthening our cosmic connection, we can learn to harness the full potential of energy and direct it toward our deepest goals and dreams.

The practice of creative visualization has ancient roots and has been used in diverse cultures throughout history. But today, more and more people are rediscovering their power and potential. Modern science supports this practice by demonstrating that our visualizations activate specific areas in our brain, thus influencing our emotions, thoughts, and even our actions.

By using creative visualization, we immerse ourselves in a state where time and space vanish, and we connect to the universal energy that flows through the entire cosmos. As we enter this heightened state of consciousness, we align with the cosmic flow, allowing us to access deeper wisdom and greater clarity.

Creative visualization becomes a powerful practice when we combine it with our innate ability to feel and experience emotions. When we visualize vividly, we immerse ourselves in the full experience, involving all of our senses and emotions. We create an energy field within us that resonates with the vibration of what we want to attract.

Let's imagine, for a moment, that we want to manifest a significant change in our lives. If we close our eyes and visualize ourselves experiencing that change, we activate our subconscious mind and intuition, which work together to help us find the path to that goal. As we allow ourselves to feel the emotions associated with that change, we raise the vibrations of our personal energy and come into resonance with what we want to attract.

Creative visualization also gives us the opportunity to explore and heal parts of ourselves that may be blocking our growth and evolution. By fully visualizing and feeling, we can identify negative thinking patterns or limiting beliefs that prevent us from moving forward. By recognizing them, we can begin the process of inner transformation and liberation, allowing us to grow to our full potential.

When we understand that we are interconnected beings in a vast and constantly evolving universe, we open ourselves to a new level of awareness. Creative visualization becomes a powerful bridge between the material and spiritual worlds, allowing us to explore and experience intuition, cosmic connection and energy balance.

In the second half of this chapter, we will delve even deeper into the practice of creative visualization and explore different techniques and approaches to enhance its effectiveness. We'll discover how we can use it to overcome obstacles, improve our manifesting abilities, and expand our cosmic connection.

We can't deny the power of creative visualization in our lives! By immersing ourselves in the art of imagining and feeling, we open ourselves to the infinite possibilities that the universe has in store for us. Let's keep going on this journey full of wonders and cosmic magic!

Creative visualization is a powerful tool that allows us to expand our cosmic connection and manifest our deepest intentions. In this second half of the chapter, we will explore different techniques and approaches that will help us to further enhance the effectiveness of creative visualization.

One of the most effective creative visualization techniques is creating a vision board. A vision board is a visual representation of our dreams, goals, and desires. To create it, we simply need a surface where we can paste images, words or phrases that represent what we want to manifest in our life. By looking at the vision board regularly, we constantly connect with our intentions and reinforce our cosmic connection.

Another powerful technique is creative meditation. During meditation, we immerse ourselves in a state of deep relaxation and open up to the experience of visualization. In this calm state, we can form clear and vivid mental images of what we wish to manifest. By combining meditation with creative visualization, we can access our subconscious more deeply and establish stronger cosmic connections.

In addition to these techniques, we can also use positive affirmations to strengthen creative visualization. Affirmations are positive statements that we repeat to reprogram our mind and align our energies with what we want to attract. By combining affirmations with clear and vivid visualizations, we are strengthening our cosmic connection and directing our energy toward our goals and dreams.

It's important to remember that creative visualization requires practice and dedication. The more we immerse ourselves in this technique, the stronger our cosmic connection will be and the easier it will be to manifest our intentions. As we continue to explore and experiment with creative visualization, we can even reach a level where our visualizations materialize in our tangible reality.

It is also essential to have patience and faith in the process. We won't always see immediate results, but with perseverance and trust, our cosmic connection will be strengthened and our intentions will be manifested in due time.

Before concluding this chapter, I want to remind you of the importance of remembering that we are interconnected beings in a vast and constantly evolving universe. Our cosmic connection is real and powerful, and creative visualization is a means by which we can explore and experience this connection in its full magnitude.

As we immerse ourselves in the art of imagining and feeling, we open the doors to a world full of infinite possibilities and cosmic wonders. Let's move forward on this journey, trusting in the wisdom of the universe and strengthening our cosmic connection through creative visualization.

In short, creative visualization invites us to explore and manifest our deepest intentions, strengthening our cosmic connection. Through techniques such as creating a vision board, creative meditation and positive affirmations, we can enhance our creative visualization and improve our ability to manifest our goals and dreams. As we continue to practice and trust the process, our visualizations will materialize in our reality, and we will open up to the infinite possibilities of the universe. In our next chapter, we will explore other forms of cosmic connection and energy balance, to continue expanding our consciousness and to live a life full of wonder and cosmic magic.

Chapter 11: Expanding Connection Through Nature

Nature is an immense treasure that gives us the opportunity to connect with something much greater than ourselves. It invites us to explore and discover the mysteries of the interconnected universe, allowing us to find balance and harmony in our vital energy. Through interaction with the natural environment, we can experience a deep and transformative cosmic connection.

When we immerse ourselves in nature, we feel a renewal of our internal energy. We let go of daily worries and open up to the wonders that surround us. The fresh air caresses our skin, the sounds of flora and fauna envelop our senses and the vibrant colors of nature invite us to a colorful dance. It is at this moment that we are aware that we are part of a larger whole, connected to the universe at its best.

Nature teaches us valuable lessons about the interconnection of all living beings. Watching plants grow and bloom reminds us of our own capacity for growth and development. Every being in nature plays a vital role in the ecosystem, just as each of us has a unique function in the fabric of life. Recognizing our own importance in this interconnected universe allows us to appreciate even more our connection to the cosmos.

By exploring and experiencing nature, we can also learn to find balance in our energy. In an increasingly fast-paced and stress-filled world, nature acts as a balm for our soul. By entering lush forests, mountainous landscapes or simply a garden, we can free our minds from everyday worries and find inner peace. The tranquility of nature helps us to balance our emotions and to tune in to the cosmic energy that flows around us.

In addition, the connection with nature invites us to be more aware of our actions and their impact on the world. As we interact with the natural environment, feelings of gratitude and responsibility to Earth, our cosmic mother, arise. We realize that our individual actions can have a significant impact on the planet's energy balance. This impels us to care for and preserve nature, not only for ourselves, but also for future generations.

Nature offers us an inexhaustible source of inspiration and wisdom. It connects us to our deepest essence and reminds us of our cosmic connection. By honoring and respecting nature, we open ourselves to the possibility of even greater cosmic expansion. As we walk along paths surrounded by ancient trees, we embark on a journey of self-exploration and spiritual growth. Nature thus becomes our teacher, guiding us on our path to a deeper cosmic connection and a lasting energy balance.

As we explore how interacting with nature can expand our cosmic connection and balance our energy, it's essential to remember that we are an integral part of this interconnected system. The next time you find yourself faced with the beauty of a sunrise or the majesty of a mountain, allow this experience to take you beyond the superficial. Immerse yourself in nature and discover the cosmic connection that awaits you. In the second half of this chapter, we'll explore practices and techniques to further expand this magical connection. Get ready to discover a new level of harmony and energy balance in the next chapter. We are waiting for you! Nature surrounds us with its magic and mystery, inviting us to immerse ourselves in its vastness and connect with the interconnected universe. In this second half of the chapter, we will expand our exploration of how interacting with nature can expand our cosmic connection and balance our energy. Follow us on this journey of self-exploration and spiritual growth.

As we enter natural spaces, we open ourselves to the possibility of discovering a deep cosmic connection with every element that surrounds us. Watch the leaves dance in the wind and the delicacy of a blossoming flower. In every detail of nature, we find fragments of the essence of the universe. As we contemplate a constantly flowing river, we are aware of the incessant cosmic energy that flows through our veins.

Nature also gives us the opportunity to balance our energy by practicing outdoor activities. Walking along a path surrounded by trees allows us to leave behind the stress and anxiety accumulated in our being. Every step-in nature is a step towards inner harmony. Listen to the birdsong and feel your spirit expand with every deep breath. The connection with nature allows you to find peace and balance in the midst of everyday chaos.

In this beautiful natural setting, we can also learn valuable lessons about the cycle of life and impermanence. Everything in nature follows a rhythm, an endless cycle of rebirth and transformation. As we observe how trees lose their leaves in autumn and recover them in spring, we are reminded of the importance of letting go and letting go of what no longer serves us. Nature teaches us that, by ceasing to hold on to what was, we can make room for new opportunities and personal growth.

We can't talk about cosmic connection through nature without mentioning the power of sacred spaces. Places such as ancient forests, majestic mountains or wild beaches have a unique energy that calls us to reconnect with our deepest essence. As we immerse ourselves in these sacred places, we become receptive to the cosmic energy that flows around us. Every step in these places is an invitation to transcendence and spiritual awakening.

The connection with nature also has a profound impact on our outlook and purpose in life. Surrounded by the vastness of nature, we realize our own smallness in the universe. This allows us to free ourselves from our egos and connect to something much bigger than ourselves. We are open to new perspectives and understand that our everyday concerns and problems are small drops compared to the vastness of the cosmos.

In this second half of the chapter, we have further explored how interacting with nature can expand our cosmic connection and balance our energy. Nature invites us to immerse ourselves in its beauty and to discover our interconnection with everything that exists. Through this connection, we find lasting energy balance and deep harmony in our lives.

So, the next time you find yourself in front of a natural landscape, allow yourself to immerse yourself in its greatness and connect with the cosmic energy that flows around you. Be aware of your role in this interconnected universe and honor nature that gives us so much. Embark on this wonderful journey of cosmic connection and energy balance that nature has to offer you!

Chapter 12: The Importance of Authenticity

Cosmic connection is a unique and mysterious experience that transcends our rational understanding. In our journey to explore the interconnected universe and energy balance, it is essential to recognize the importance of authenticity. Being authentic strengthens our cosmic connection and allows us to maintain a healthy energy balance.

In a world where we are often encouraged to follow social expectations and to fit into certain molds, being authentic can seem like a challenge. However, it is in our authenticity that we find our power and true essence. When we allow ourselves to be who we really are, we transcend imposed limitations and connect with a greater force.

Authenticity invites us to question the beliefs and thought patterns we have acquired throughout our lives. It asks us to step away from the masks we wear to please others and immerse ourselves in the truth of our being. In doing so, we release a vital energy that flows in harmony with the whole, nourishing our cosmic connection.

By being authentic, we open the doors to the manifestation of our purpose and our true passion. We allow ourselves to live aligned with our true nature and express our unique gifts and talents. This alignment is essential for maintaining a healthy energy balance, as it triggers a series of positive reactions in our body, mind and spirit.

When we act from a place of authenticity, our actions and decisions are in line with our deepest values. We become aware of our emotional and physical needs, and we strive to meet them in a balanced way. This creates a constant flow of vital energy into our being, allowing us to face external challenges with greater resilience and clarity of purpose.

However, authenticity is not a static goal, but rather a journey of self-discovery and continuous growth. It requires courage and willingness to face our shadows and learn from them. Often, life experiences lead us to move away from our authenticity, but there are always opportunities to return to it and reconnect with our essence.

Authenticity also invites us to cultivate meaningful and genuine relationships with others. When we are authentic, we allow other people to come to us from an authentic place as well. We connect in a deeper vibration and create bonds based on mutual understanding and sincere support. These sincere relationships nourish us and strengthen our cosmic connection.

As we continue to explore the importance of authenticity in our cosmic connection and in maintaining a healthy energy balance, we realize that being authentic is an act of self-love. We give ourselves the freedom to be who we really are and open ourselves to the expansive experience of the interconnected universe.

In the second half of this chapter, we'll explore practices and reflections that will help us cultivate authenticity in our daily lives. We will discover ways to overcome challenges and obstacles that may arise on our path to authenticity, and we will delve deeper into the transformative impact this has on our cosmic connection and energy balance.

We'll delve into the cosmic dance of authenticity and explore how this powerful link with our true essence guides us to a sense of wholeness and purpose. Join us on this journey to authenticity and discover how to strengthen your cosmic connection and maintain a healthy energy balance. In this second half of the chapter, we will continue our journey to authenticity and immerse ourselves in practices and reflections that will help us cultivate it in our daily lives. We will discover how to overcome the challenges and obstacles that may appear on our path to authenticity, and we will delve into the transformative impact this has on our cosmic connection and energy balance.

One of the keys to cultivating authenticity is learning to listen to and trust our inner voice. We often let ourselves be carried away by the expectations and opinions of others, which take us away from our most authentic essence. Taking the time to connect with our inner being helps us to attune to our true needs and wants. This involves cultivating the practice of mindfulness and personal reflection in our daily lives.

Mindfulness allows us to connect to the present moment without judgment or distraction. By paying attention to our thoughts, emotions, and physical sensations, we can more easily identify when we are acting or making decisions outside of our authenticity. When this happens, we give ourselves permission to pause and evaluate whether our actions are aligned with our deepest values.

In addition to mindfulness, personal reflection is essential for cultivating authenticity. By taking time to reflect on our experiences and experiences, we can learn from them and nurture our personal growth. Questions like "What do I really want in life?", "What are my deepest values?" and "What am I really passionate about?" help us gain clarity about who we are and what drives us.

As we deepen our authenticity, we may face challenges and obstacles along the way. We may be met with resistance from those who expect us to follow the conventional path or social expectations. In these moments, it's essential to remember that our authenticity is a gift that only we can give to ourselves and to the world.

Let us remember that authenticity is an act of self-love. It is a commitment to ourselves to live a life consistent with our innermost truths. Although it may seem difficult at times, the path to authenticity rewards us with a greater sense of wholeness and cosmic connection.

In addition, as we cultivate our authenticity, we also open the door to the possibility of inspiring others to do the same. Our genuine and sincere actions can serve as a beacon of light for those who are in search of their own authenticity. Sharing our journey allows us to build meaningful and authentic relationships with those who resonate with our true essence.

In conclusion, the importance of authenticity lies in its ability to strengthen our cosmic connection and maintain a healthy energy balance. Cultivating authenticity allows us to live aligned with our true nature, express our unique gifts, and meet our needs in a balanced way. Throughout this chapter, we have explored authenticity as a journey of self-discovery and continuous growth, full of challenges and opportunities to reconnect with our essence.

Now I invite you to dive into your own journey to authenticity. Allow yourself to be who you really are, releasing your vital energy and connecting with the vast interconnected universe that surrounds us. As you open up to the expansive experience of authenticity, you'll discover how to strengthen your cosmic connection and maintain a healthy energy balance.

Chapter 13: Cosmic Connections Through Art and Creativity.

Exploring the interconnected universe and energy balance leads us to countless paths of knowledge and understanding. On our journey to a deeper connection with the cosmos, we discover that art and creativity play a fundamental role. Through them, we enter a world full of infinite possibilities, where our souls are intertwined with the vastness of the universe.

Art and creativity are genuine expressions of who we are, a way to release our deepest thoughts and emotions. When we immerse ourselves in the creative process, we connect with a universal energy that flows through us, as if we were being channeled by invisible forces. At that moment, our creations transcend their physical form and take on a life of their own, carrying with them the very essence of the cosmos.

By exploring art and creativity from a cosmic perspective, we discover how these expressions open us to a new dimension of connection. We become part of the fabric of the universe, a cosmic entanglement that is manifested through our works. Every stroke, every note and every idea bring us closer to the deepest mysteries of the universe.

Throughout history, many artists and thinkers have explored this relationship between art, creativity and the cosmos. From the ancient Greeks to the Renaissance masters, we find a constant quest to understand the beauty and harmony found in all things. These creators perceived the intrinsic connection between the physical and spiritual worlds, and used art as a tool to explore and communicate these universal truths.

Art invites us to look beyond the surface and enter the deepest realms of our existence. When we immerse ourselves in a work of art, our senses awaken and our perception expands. It's as if we can feel the heartbeat of the universe, hear its whispered secrets, and see its mysteries revealed before our eyes. We become witnesses and active participants in the dance of creation.

Creativity also allows us to explore our own internal energy and harmonize it with universal energy. When we let ourselves be carried away by the creative flow, we allow our minds and hearts to be shaped by forces greater than ourselves. We are in a state of grace, where our ideas and actions flow in sync with the rhythm of the cosmos. In this state, we are not only recipients of cosmic energy, but we also become transmitters of that energy.

As we immerse ourselves in the exploration of art and creativity as a gateway to the cosmos, we discover that our creations not only connect us to the divine, but also connect us to ourselves and to others. As we share our creations with the world, we establish an invisible network of connections, uniting through the common experience of beauty and expression.

Cosmic connection through art and creativity is an endless journey. As we continue to explore and create, we enter unknown territories where barriers vanish and we find ourselves completely immersed in cosmic energy. It is through this process that we find an authentic alignment with the universe, a deep resonance that allows us to be an integral part of the whole.

In the second half of this chapter, we will delve into how we can use art and creativity to strengthen our cosmic connection and harmonize our energy. We will explore practices and techniques that will help us to open up to the higher frequencies of the cosmos and to discover our true essence in the creative process. We will also explore how our creations can act as bridges between dimensions, taking us to unimaginable places where reality and fantasy are intertwined. Get ready to embark on an unprecedented journey of discovery and expansion! The cosmic connection we experience through art and creativity leads us to a state of unity, where our souls merge with the extraordinary wonders of the universe. In this second half of the chapter, we'll explore additional techniques and practices that allow us to delve even deeper into our cosmic connection and harmonize our energy.

One of the most powerful ways to strengthen our cosmic connection through art and creativity is through meditation. Calming our minds and opening ourselves to the wisdom of the universe allows us to access new ideas and creative visions. As we meditate, we immerse ourselves in an ocean of cosmic energy, allowing inspiration to flow through us. The images and sounds that we experience in a meditative state can be transformed into artistic creations that emanate a deep cosmic resonance.

Another powerful practice is creative visualization. By entering a state of visualization, we open ourselves to a space were reality merges with imagination. We can vividly imagine what it's like to be in connection with the universe, how we feel when our souls dance in harmony with the stars. Visualizing our creations and artistic projects as expressions of the cosmos allows us to infuse them with a unique and transcendental energy.

The use of symbols and metaphors in art and creativity can also lead us to a deeper connection with the cosmos. Symbols have been used throughout history as a form of communication with the divine. Through symbols, we can transmit and receive cosmic messages, revealing truths and ideas that transcend conventional language. By using symbols in our creations, we can explore the multiple layers of meaning that exist in the universe and express our connection to it in a unique and personal way.

In addition, music and sound play a fundamental role in our cosmic connection through art and creativity. Rhythm and melody allow us to tune in to the vibrations of the universe, transporting us to a heightened state of consciousness. Cosmic music, created with the intention of opening us up to the vastness of the cosmos, can help us release blocked energies and align our bodies, minds and spirits with the highest frequencies in the universe.

Finally, interaction with other artists and creatives can enrich our cosmic connection. By sharing our creations and exploring the works of others, we establish a network of cosmic connections that allows us to collaborate and grow together. As we unite with other human beings in a creative act, we realize that we are nodes in a wonderful cosmic web, all connected and in resonance with one another.

In short, art and creativity are gateways to cosmic connection. As we explore and immerse ourselves in the creative process, we come closer to a true alignment with the universe, where our creations become a testament to our participation in the fabric of existence. Through meditation, visualization, the use of symbols, music and sound, as well as interacting with other creatives, we can expand our cosmic connection and harmonize our energy with the higher frequencies of the cosmos.

In our next chapter, we'll explore how we can transfer cosmic energy and connection beyond art and creativity to other aspects of our lives. We'll discover how we can incorporate wisdom and cosmic resonance into our intimacy, our relationships, and our daily actions. Get ready to continue on this journey toward cosmic connection and energy balance!

Chapter 14: The Power of Speech and Conscious Communication

Communication is one of the most powerful and fundamental tools we have as human beings. Through words, we are able to express our emotions, ideas and thoughts, establishing connections with others and establishing meaningful interaction in the world around us. However, we are not always aware of the impact that our words and our communication have on our own consciousness and on our cosmic connection.

Every word we utter has an inherent power, whether to create or destroy, to uplift or restrict, to connect or disconnect. Our words are energy in motion, vibrations that are transmitted through time and space, and that have the potential to influence our reality and the reality of those around us.

Conscious communication involves being fully aware of the words we use and how we use them. It requires deep introspection and a connection with our inner being to choose our words wisely and consciously. When we become aware of our word, we open up to a deeper level of understanding and connection with ourselves and with the universe.

By consciously expressing ourselves, we realize that our words are loaded with intent. Every word we utter is like a seed that we plant in the field of reality, and depending on the seed we choose, we will reap the corresponding fruits. If our words are filled with love, compassion and gratitude, we will create an environment of harmony and positive connections. On the contrary, if our words are filled with judgment, resentment, or criticism, we will cultivate a terrain full of discord and emotional detachment.

Our consciousness is intrinsically linked to our words and to how we communicate. If we consciously choose our words, we become co-creators of our reality and of the reality that we share with others. Our words can act as a guide to manifest our desires and dreams, but they can also limit us and keep us stuck in negative patterns.

In our cosmic connection, our words are a means of establishing a bridge between us and the universe. Through conscious communication, we become channels of energy and knowledge, transmitting and receiving valuable information. When we use our words to express our authentic truth and to communicate from the heart, we align ourselves with cosmic energies and become instruments of change and transformation.

To improve our conscious communication and strengthen our cosmic connection, it's vital to practice active listening. Active listening involves being fully present in the moment, paying full attention to the other's words and to the non-verbal signals they transmit to us. By actively listening, we open ourselves to the possibility of truly understanding others, establishing a deep and meaningful connection.

In addition, we must be aware of how our words can affect others. Every person has their own unique experiences and perspectives, so it's important to consider how our words can be received by others. Being respectful, compassionate, and empathetic in our communication will help us build stronger, more meaningful relationships, and foster an environment of mutual understanding and personal growth.

Therefore, I invite you to be aware of the power of your words and how you communicate with others. Allow yourself to be a channel of love, compassion, and wisdom in your daily interactions. See how your words can influence your own consciousness and your cosmic connection. In the second part of this chapter, we will explore practical strategies to improve our conscious communication and enhance our connection to the interconnected universe. Get ready to discover the incredible power of words and conscious communication in your life!

(It includes an interruption and leaves the end of the sentence open for the second part of the chapter without explicitly mentioning it) The second part of this chapter will focus on exploring practical strategies and tools to improve our conscious communication and further enhance our connection to the interconnected universe. Here are some of the practices you can implement in your daily life to cultivate more conscious and powerful communication:

1. The practice of mindfulness: Mindfulness is an invaluable tool for improving the quality of our communication. By practicing mindfulness, we learn to be fully present in the moment and to pay full attention to our words and to the words of others. This allows us to avoid responding automatically or impulsively, and instead, to respond consciously and authentically.

2. Clarity in expression: It's important to be clear and precise when expressing our ideas and emotions. This involves using simple and direct language, avoiding ambiguity or vagueness. By being clear in our expression, we facilitate understanding by others and avoid misunderstandings.

3. Active, empathetic listening: Active listening involves being fully present and paying attention to the other person's words and nonverbal language. In addition, empathy allows us to truly understand the perspective and experiences of the other. By practicing active and empathetic listening, we create a safe and trusting space where both can freely express themselves and be understood.

4. The practice of non-violence in communication: Conscious communication involves moving away from verbal violence or any form of communication that causes harm or suffering. We must be aware of our words, avoiding insult, destructive criticism, or judgment. Instead, we must seek constructive and loving ways to express ourselves.

5. Assertive communication: Being assertive involves expressing our needs, emotions and opinions in a respectful and direct way. It's important to learn to communicate clearly and firmly, without aggressiveness or passivity. Assertive communication allows us to set healthy boundaries and build more genuine and balanced relationships.

6. The practice of gratitude and appreciation: Expressing gratitude and appreciation to others is a powerful way to strengthen our connections and create an environment of harmony. By consciously communicating from a state of gratitude, we raise the vibrations of our communication and establish a positive energy field.

These are just a few of the many strategies we can use to improve our conscious communication and strengthen our connection to the interconnected universe. As we integrate these practices into our daily interactions, we will begin to experience a profound transformation in our relationships and in our own consciousness.

Remember that speech and conscious communication are powerful tools that allow us to co-create our reality and express our most authentic truth. Allow yourself to explore and discover the incredible potential of your conscious communication in all aspects of your life.

In the next chapter, we'll explore the role of intuition and cosmic connection in our conscious communication. Get ready to dive into a journey of inner exploration and discover the magic of cosmic connection through our words and conscious communication!

Chapter 15: The Importance of Mindful Eating

Mindful eating is a concept that invites us to reflect on the importance of how we eat and how this can nourish our cosmic connection and balance our energy. In a fast-paced world full of distractions, we often forget the importance of paying attention to what we eat and how it affects us physically, mentally and spiritually.

When we talk about cosmic connection, we refer to that sacred connection that exists between the universe and us as human beings. We are part of an interconnected whole and, by being aware of this, we can cultivate a deep harmony in our being. Mindful eating offers us a powerful tool to achieve this.

In our daily lives, most of the time we simply eat without paying attention. We run from place to place, pecking on fast and processed foods, without really taking into account the nutrients we are consuming and how this impacts our body. It's as if we're disconnected from what we're eating and how our food choices can affect us physically and emotionally.

However, when we take a moment to be aware of each bite, to appreciate the taste and texture of food, we are generating a profound change in our relationship with food. By doing so, we open ourselves to the possibility of experiencing a deeper connection with nature and with our own being.

Mindful eating also involves paying attention to our own bodies and individual needs. Each of us is unique, and so are our nutritional needs.

By being aware of our physical sensations, we are able to identify the foods that really nourish us and provide us with quality energy.

The quality of the food we consume has a direct impact on our energy balance. By choosing fresh, organic and seasonal foods, we are nourishing our bodies with the vital energy that nature provides us. On the contrary, processed foods full of chemical additives lead us to an energy imbalance that is reflected in our mood, our health and our cosmic connection.

In this process of conscious eating, it is also important to cultivate a relationship of gratitude to food and to the universe that provides it to us. Appreciating every bite and recognizing the abundance and generosity of nature helps us connect with a higher energy and nourish our cosmic connection.

In short, mindful eating is a journey of self-discovery and connection with the divine that surrounds us. It invites us to pay attention to what we eat, to nourish our body with foods that provide us with quality energy, and to cultivate a relationship of gratitude towards food and nature. In doing so, we open ourselves to an experience of cosmic connection and energy balance that can profoundly transform our lives.

The practice of mindful eating allows us to reconnect with our essence and balance our energies in a deep and meaningful way. By paying attention to what we eat and how it affects us, we can make a difference in our physical, mental and spiritual health. In this second half of the chapter, we'll explore how we can implement mindful eating into our daily lives and the benefits this can bring us.

One of the most effective ways to begin practicing mindful eating is to pay attention to our physical and emotional sensations. How do we feel before, during and after our meals? Which foods provide us with energy and vitality, and which ones leave us feeling exhausted or unwell? Taking note of these things helps us identify what foods are right for us and which we should limit or avoid.

In addition, it's important to take the time to plan our meals and prepare them with love and care. By cooking our own food, we are in control of the ingredients we use and can ensure that they are fresh, natural and nutritious. This not only allows us to nourish our body with quality food, but it also connects us to gratitude for the ingredients and the nature that provides them.

Conscious food choices also involve respecting and honoring our connection to the environment. Opting for organic, seasonal food is one way to support sustainable agricultural practices and reduce our ecological footprint. By doing so, we are helping to preserve the health of the planet and to feed ourselves in harmony with nature.

Another way to deepen mindful eating is to practice moderation and balance. It's not about following restrictive diets or counting calories, but about developing a healthy relationship with food. When we learn to listen to our body and respect its signals of hunger and satiety, we can meet our nutritional needs without falling into patterns of compulsive or restrictive eating.

In addition, mindful eating invites us to slow down and enjoy every bite. Many times, we eat in a hurry, without paying attention to the taste and texture of the food. However, by eating slowly and mindfully, we can more fully appreciate the sensory qualities of food. This not only allows us to enjoy our meals more, but it also helps us to better digest food and absorb its nutrients.

Finally, gratitude continues to play a critical role in mindful eating. Being thankful for the food we have on our plate and for the abundance that surrounds us connects us to greater spiritual awareness. In doing so, we open ourselves to an experience of deeper cosmic connection and cultivate gratitude as a constant state of being.

In conclusion, mindful eating is a path to comprehensive well-being. By taking the time to reflect on how we eat and how this affects our connection with the divine, we can transform our relationship with food and with ourselves. The practice of mindful eating helps us to nourish our body, balance our energies and be in harmony with the universe that surrounds us. May this reflection inspire us to adopt conscious eating and experience the transformative benefits that this can bring us.

Chapter 16: Connecting to the Cosmos through Music and Sound

Music and sound are elements that have been present in our lives since time immemorial. They have resonated in our ears and have left a deep imprint on our emotions and thoughts. But beyond their impact on the earthly sphere, what role do they play in our relationship with the cosmos? How can they act as bridges to a deeper connection with the universe and our energy balance?

To understand the connection between music, sound and the cosmos, it's important to delve into the very nature of sound. Every sound we perceive is nothing more than a vibration, a wave of energy that spreads and reaches our ears. This basic essence of sound is what allows us to establish a link with the cosmos, since the universe is also in constant vibration.

Throughout history, different cultures have recognized the importance of music and sound as a means to connect with the divine, with the universe. From ancient indigenous civilizations to Eastern philosophies, there is a deep understanding of how these elements can be used to achieve a state of harmony and balance.

Music, in its purest essence, is capable of transporting us to a higher dimension. It immerses us in an ocean of emotions and allows us to escape from everyday reality to enter a world of unique sensations. When listening to a melody, we can feel that our internal vibrations are synchronized with those of the universe, creating a cosmic connection.

But it's not just music created by others that has this transformative power. Anyone can explore their own ability to create music and sounds.

It is through musical creation that we can experience a deeper connection with our cosmic environment. By giving life to our own sounds, we open a door to our interior and to the connection with the universe.

Music has also been used as a tool to enhance meditation and the state of consciousness. The right rhythms and melodies can help us achieve greater concentration and move us into a state of calm and mental clarity. The practice of conscious music, in which we immerse ourselves in creating sounds with full attention and presence, allows us to establish a deep connection with the cosmos and our innermost essence.

In line with music, sound also plays a fundamental role in our cosmic exploration. From the sounds of nature, such as the wind and the waves of the sea, to the sound of ancient instruments, such as Tibetan bowls and shamanic drums, each of them offers us a channel to connect with the universe in its most basic form.

The vibration of these sounds envelops us in an energy that guides us to states of introspection and expansion of consciousness. By immersing ourselves in sound, we allow the barriers of the mind to dissolve and we open up to a universe of infinite possibilities. It's as if the sound reminds us that we are part of something much bigger, that our individual vibrations are intertwined with those of the cosmos to create a universal symphony.

In this first approach to cosmic connection through music and sound, we have explored how these elements act as bridges to a deeper connection with the universe and our energy balance. Music transports us to higher dimensions and synchronizes us with the vibrations of the cosmos, while sound immerses us in an ancient energy that amplifies our perception and guides us to new horizons.

In the second half of this chapter, we will delve into the specific practices that allow us to experience this cosmic connection through music and sound. We will explore the therapeutic applications, meditation techniques and sacred rituals that help us open the doors of our being to the interconnected universe. Get ready to embark on a journey of self-discovery and expansion of consciousness through music and sound. In the second half of this chapter, we will delve into specific practices that will allow us to experience a deeper cosmic connection through music and sound. We will explore therapeutic applications, meditation techniques and sacred rituals that will help us open the doors of our being to the interconnected universe.

One of the most powerful ways to use music and sound as vehicles to a cosmic connection is through the practice of sound meditation. This technique invites us to immerse ourselves in the peace and serenity that comes from the vibration of sounds. By focusing on music or the sounds of sacred instruments, such as Tibetan bowls, fretboards, or shamanic drums, we can experience a deep state of relaxation and connection with our inner being.

During sound meditation, we allow sounds to enter our consciousness and immerse us in a unique sensory experience. As we let the vibrations resonate in our body, a synchronization occurs between our individual energy and that of the cosmos. This brings us to a state of harmony and balance, where we feel connected to everything around us.

Another technique that helps us connect with the cosmos through music and sound is the chanting of mantras. Mantras are repetitions of sacred words or phrases that help us to center our mind and focus our attention on the divine. By chanting mantras, we release energy through our bodies and our sounds become a channel for communicating with the universe.

The practice of chanting mantras allows us to open our hearts and minds to the cosmic essence that dwells within us. As we repeat the mantras over and over again, we immerse ourselves in their deep meaning and connect with an ancient wisdom that guides us to transcendence. Mantras not only help us find peace and healing, but they also allow us to raise our vibrations and tune in to the frequency of the universe.

In addition to meditation and the chanting of mantras, there are sacred rituals that allow us to experience a cosmic connection through music and sound. These rituals are used by various ancient cultures to honor the gods and connect with the divine. They can involve dances, songs, the playing of sacred instruments and other elements that transport us to a state of deep devotion and spiritual elevation.

By participating in sacred rituals, we open ourselves to the experience of being part of something greater than ourselves. We connect with the cosmic energy that flows through all beings and allow ourselves to be guided by the ancient wisdom that has been transmitted from generation to generation. These rituals help us to recognize our intrinsic connection to the universe and to live in harmony with it.

In short, music and sound are powerful tools that allow us to experience a deeper cosmic connection. Through sound meditation, the chanting of mantras and sacred rituals, we can open the doors of our being to the interconnected universe. By immersing ourselves in the vibration of sounds, we synchronize with the cosmos and experience a state of harmony and balance. Get ready to embark on a journey of self-discovery and expansion of consciousness through music and sound.

Chapter 17: The Importance of Living in the Present

Throughout our lives, we find ourselves stuck between two points in time: the past and the future. However, it is in the present that the true power of connection with the cosmos and energy balance resides. Living in the here and now allows us to experience the fullness of each moment, recognizing that we are beings interconnected with the universe and that energy flows through us.

In a fast-paced and constantly distracted world, we often find ourselves stuck in thoughts about what happened in the past or worried about what the future holds. We hold on to past memories and experiences, allowing them to shape the way we think and act in the present. In the same way, we lose ourselves in worries and yearnings for the future, leaving aside the opportunities that present themselves to us in the present.

The reality is that the past no longer exists and the future has not yet arrived. We only have control and the ability to fully experience the present. This is where our cosmic connection is strengthened and where we can find a lasting energy balance. By living in the present, we open ourselves to the vastness of the universe that surrounds us and recognize our interconnection with everything around us.

To live fully in the present, it's essential to practice mindfulness. Mindfulness is the ability to be consciously present in every moment, without judging or clinging to the thoughts or emotions that arise. Through mindfulness, we can attune to the cosmic energy that flows around us, allowing it to guide and balance us.

As we engage with the cosmos through mindfulness, we become more aware of the signs and synchronicities that surround us. We begin to recognize the patterns in our lives and how we are connected to the universal flow of energy. This recognition gives us greater understanding and wisdom, allowing us to make decisions that are more aligned with our true essence and purpose.

The importance of living in the present also lies in our ability to stay in harmony with our own internal energy. Sometimes, our minds can be overwhelmed by noise and external expectations, leading us to lose that internal balance. However, by living in the present, we can tune in to our internal energy and learn to recognize what serves and nourishes us.

By being present, we also allow ourselves to fully experience our emotions and feelings without judging them or labeling them as good or bad. We open ourselves to cosmic connection and energy balance when we accept ourselves and all parts of our being.

In short, living in the present is a practice that allows us to be more connected to the cosmos and in balance with our energy. Through mindfulness and acceptance of ourselves, we open the door to a deeper connection with the universe and to the fullness of every moment. The magic of the present awaits us, ready to be discovered and experienced, keeping our essence in harmony with the cosmos.

By practicing mindfulness and living in the present, we can experience a profound transformation in our lives. We find ourselves more connected to the cosmos and in balance with our energy. But how can we incorporate this approach into our daily lives?

One way to cultivate mindfulness is through meditation. Taking a few moments each day to sit in silence, close our eyes, and focus our attention on our breathing allows us to calm our minds and be present in the present moment. As we practice this regularly, we develop the ability to bring that mindfulness to our daily activities.

By performing everyday tasks, such as washing dishes, walking, or simply having a cup of tea, we can fully practice mindfulness. We pay attention to every movement, every sensation and every thought that comes up. We become aware of our senses: the scent of soap, the feeling of water in our hands, the taste of hot tea. We stay immersed in the present, savoring every moment.

Another way of living in the present is through connection with nature. When we delve into nature, whether taking a walk in the forest or simply looking at a beautiful landscape, we can experience a deep connection with the cosmos. Nature teaches us the importance of being rooted in the now, of flowing in harmony with universal cycles. It shows us the beauty and perfection of every present moment.

In addition, it is essential to learn to let go of attachment to the past and to the future. Recognizing that the past can no longer be changed and that the future is uncertain allows us to focus on the present. Freeing ourselves from expectations and transcending regrets or fears allows us to be fully present and open to the opportunities that come our way.

Living in the present also involves cultivating gratitude for everything we are and everything we have right now. Often, we focus on what we lack or what we want to achieve in the future, losing sight of the blessings and gifts that are already present in our lives. By practicing gratitude, we focus on the now and connect with the abundance that surrounds us.

In addition, it's important to remember that living in the present doesn't mean denying the past or ignoring planning for the future. It's healthy to reflect on and learn from our history, as well as to set goals and take action to create the future we want. However, the key is to recognize that all of this is done from a solid foundation in the present.

By living in the present, we open ourselves to the magic and beauty that surrounds us. We connect with the cosmos, allowing its energy to flow through us and guide us every step of the way. We release the stress and anxiety that come from being stuck in the past or worried about the future. We become conscious and empowered beings, capable of making decisions aligned with our true essence.

In conclusion, the importance of living in the present lies in our connection with the cosmos and our energy balance. Through mindfulness, connecting with nature, letting go of attachment and gratitude, we can experience the fullness of every moment. Let us embrace the magic of the present, accepting and living every moment with gratitude and presence, thus finding our place in the interconnected universe.

Chapter 18: The Cosmic Connection and the Purpose of Life

In this chapter, we dive into a deep journey to explore how our cosmic connection is closely related to finding and living our purpose in life. As we deepen our understanding of our interconnected universe and the energy balance that surrounds it, we will discover how our own experiences and choices are intrinsically linked to a greater purpose.

Each of us is part of a vast and complex cosmic fabric, in which all things are connected. From the stars that light up our night sky to the atoms that make up our bodies, everything in the universe is interconnected in a mysterious and beautiful way. This cosmic connection transcends physical barriers and extends into the realms of energy and consciousness.

As we reflect on our existence in this vast cosmos, it's natural to ask ourselves what our purpose is in this life. Why are we here? What is the meaning behind our experiences and challenges? Seeking answers to these questions leads us to explore the deep relationship between our cosmic connection and our purpose in life.

When we look at the intricate nature of our universe, from the way planets orbit the sun to the way cells work together in our bodies, we realize that there is an underlying order and harmony in everything. In the same way, each of us has a unique role to play in this cosmic dance.

Finding our purpose in life involves attuning ourselves to the energy of the universe and listening attentively to the signals that come to us. These signs can manifest as passions and talents, as an internal call that drives us towards certain activities or professions. By connecting with our deepest essence and aligning ourselves with cosmic resonance, we discover how our individual existence fits into the great puzzle of the universe.

Our cosmic connection also encompasses interaction with other human beings. As we relate to others and share our gifts and talents, we create networks of support and mutual growth. In this sense, our cosmic connection is manifested through relationships and the impact we have on the lives of others.

The journey toward understanding our cosmic connection and finding our life purpose may not be an easy path. Often, we face obstacles and challenges that cause us to question our direction and our meaning in this vast universe. However, it is in these moments of uncertainty that we can discover deep inner strength and a connection to the power of the universe.

As we move forward in exploring this cosmic connection and its relationship to our purpose in life, it's critical to remember that each of us has a unique and valuable role in the cosmic fabric. Our lives are a reflection of the interconnectedness and interdependence that exists in the universe.

In the second part of this chapter, we will further explore how we can cultivate our cosmic connection and use it to discover and live our purpose in life. We will delve into practices and tools that will help us to attune to cosmic resonance and to find clarity in our individual paths. Get ready to dive even deeper into the interconnected universe and unveil the power of your purpose. The journey continues, and we are about to discover the wonders that await us as we explore our cosmic connection and the purpose of life. As we dive into the journey of exploring our cosmic connection and the purpose of life, we encounter challenges and moments of uncertainty that lead us to question our direction in this vast universe. However, these obstacles should not discourage us, but rather, they should serve as opportunities to discover our deep inner strength and our connection to the power of the universe.

When faced with moments of uncertainty, it's essential to remember that each of us has a unique and valuable role in the cosmic fabric. Our lives are a manifestation of the interconnectedness and interdependence that exists in the universe. Every choice and experience we go through has a purpose and contributes to the energy balance of the cosmos.

To cultivate our cosmic connection and find clarity in our individual paths, it's important to tune in to cosmic resonance and learn to listen to the signals that come to us. The universe is constantly speaking to us through our passions, talents, and inner callings. We must be attentive to these signs and allow them to guide us towards our purpose in life.

A powerful tool for connecting with our cosmic resonance is meditation. Through meditation, we can enter into a state of calm and stillness, allowing us to hear our inner voice and receive the wisdom and guidance of the universe. By dedicating time to meditation, we can dispel confusion and find clarity in our purposes and objectives.

In addition to meditation, another effective practice for cultivating our cosmic connection is the observation of nature. By delving into the beauty and harmony of nature, we can find inspiration and better understand our place in the universe. Observing the cycles of life in nature, from the blossoming of a flower to the birth of a new being, reminds us of the intrinsic connection between all forms of life and helps us to appreciate even more our cosmic interconnection.

It's also important to surround ourselves with people who support us on our journey toward understanding our cosmic connection and purpose in life. By interacting with other human beings who share our search for meaning, we can grow together and find mutual inspiration. Sharing our experiences, challenges and triumphs helps us develop a support network that supports us every step of the way.

As we move on our journey to a greater understanding of our cosmic connection and our purpose in life, it's critical to keep an open mind and be willing to learn and grow. The universe is vast and complex, and there's always more to discover. We must not hold on to preconceived ideas or self-imposed limitations. Instead, we must be open to new perspectives and willing to adapt and evolve in our understanding of the world.

This journey of exploring our cosmic connection and the purpose of life is a lifelong quest. Every day is an opportunity to deepen our understanding and discover new wonders in the interconnected universe. As we connect more and more to cosmic resonance, we find a sense of wholeness and purpose that transcends our individual lives.

In our cosmic connection and in the search for our purpose in life, we find a deep connection with the universe and with ourselves. We are an integral part of this cosmic fabric, and by embracing our connection, we unlock the power and unlimited potential that we all carry within.

So, continue on this journey of self-exploration and cosmic connection, exploring the wonders that await you in the search for your life purpose. Remember, every step you take brings closer to understanding your place in the universe and to realizing your purpose. Keep believing in yourself and never forget that you are a valuable and unique cosmic being. The universe patiently waits for your intuition and your choices to show you the path to the realization of your cosmic destiny. Enter the second part of this chapter with courage and confidence, the answers you are looking for are closer than you imagine!

Chapter 19: The Art of Letting Go and Trusting the Universe

Life is a constant flow of energies and cosmic connections that surround and surround us, and when we learn to let go of resistance and trust the universe, we can experience a deep connection and energy balance in our lives.

Throughout our existence, we tend to hold on to situations, people, and emotions that are familiar and comfortable to us. Resistance becomes our natural response to change and the unknown. However, in this chapter we will explore how letting go of that resistance and opening ourselves to trust in the universe gives us the opportunity to be more connected and energetically balanced.

When we resist the natural flow of life, we find ourselves in a constant state of struggle and tension. We hold on to our expectations and desires, trying to control every aspect of our existence. But what if instead of holding on, we learned to let go and trust the universe?

By letting go of resistance, we release the weight of our expectations and allow life to unfold smoothly and naturally. Instead of fighting against the currents, we learn to let ourselves be carried away by them, trusting that the universe will always guide us to our most authentic path.

The key is to surrender to the present moment, to live in full consciousness and to accept what life presents to us. As we let go of our resistance, we find an inner calm that allows us to flow in harmony with the universe. We no longer resist change, but instead embrace them as opportunities for growth and transformation.

By trusting the universe, we recognize that we are part of something much larger than ourselves. We connect with universal wisdom and intelligence, and we understand that everything that happens to us has a higher purpose. Every challenge, every obstacle, becomes valuable learning on our journey to wholeness.

Trust in the universe doesn't mean being passive or stopping striving for what we want. Rather, it involves letting go of control and trusting that, as we open ourselves to the opportunities present in our path, the universe will conspire in our favor. By being attuned to our intuition and our inner needs, we can make decisions that will lead us to our true happiness.

When we let go of resistance and trust the universe, we open ourselves to the possibility of a deeper connection with ourselves and with others. Energy flows freely through us, allowing us to experience a sense of wholeness and harmony in our relationships, our health, and our purpose in life.

In short, letting go of resistance and trusting the universe allows us to be more connected and in energy balance. By freeing ourselves from our expectations and clings, we can flow with life flexibly and authentically. Trust in the universe gives us the opportunity to connect with our true essence and experience profound transformation. In the next chapter, we'll explore practical tools to cultivate this trust and release resistance in our daily lives. Continued...

By letting go of resistance and trusting the universe, we open ourselves to the possibility of a deeper connection with ourselves and with others. Energy flows freely through us, allowing us to experience a sense of wholeness and harmony in our relationships, our health, and our purpose in life.

When we trust the universe, we also learn to trust ourselves. We recognize that we have the internal capacity to overcome any obstacle and to make decisions aligned with our true essence. We become aware of our abilities and free ourselves from the fears and doubts that limit us.

Trust in the universe invites us to be patient and to flow with the natural rhythm of life. We understand that things happen at the perfect time and that every experience, whether good or bad, teaches us something valuable. We don't resist challenges, but face them with courage and confidence that we can transform them into opportunities for growth.

In addition, by letting go of resistance, we release attachment to results. We learn to enjoy the process and to accept that the final result may be different from what we imagined. This does not mean that we stop having goals and dreams, but rather that we trust that the universe will guide us in the right direction.

Trust in the universe connects us to a force greater than ourselves. It helps us recognize that we are part of an interconnected cosmic fabric, in which our actions and intentions have an impact on the entire universe. With this awareness, our decisions become more conscious and aligned with the well-being of all.

On this journey of letting go and trusting the universe, it's important to remember that we're not alone. We have the support and guidance of forces beyond our comprehension. Whether through synchronicities, signs or messages, the universe always offers us signs to remind us that we are on the right path.

By cultivating trust in the universe, we learn to listen to our intuition and to follow our truest passions. We allow ourselves to be vulnerable and open to the experiences that life presents to us. We learn to let go of control and to flow with the currents, trusting that we are following the right path.

In conclusion, the art of letting go and trusting the universe gives us the opportunity to live in a state of deep connection and energy balance. By freeing ourselves from resistance and relying on our inner wisdom and the forces of the universe, we can experience profound transformation in all areas of our lives.

The next chapter will explore practical tools to further cultivate this trust and release resistance in our daily lives. We'll discover meditative practices, powerful affirmations, and strategies to stay connected to ourselves and to the universe. Get ready to embark on a journey of self-discovery and transformation as we learn to embrace the art of letting go and trusting the universe.

Remember, the power is in your hands and in your ability to trust that the universe is always conspiring in your favor.

Chapter 20: Integrating Cosmic Connection into Our Daily Lives

Modern life can be hectic and challenging. We find ourselves immersed in a constant whirlwind of responsibilities, demands and distractions that often take us away from our true essence and disconnect us from the interconnected universe that surrounds us. However, within that daily hustle and bustle, we can find ways to integrate cosmic connection into our lives and maintain a constant energy balance.

To get started, it's essential that we take the time necessary to connect with ourselves. In the midst of the hustle and bustle of our days, we can forget the importance of self-exploration and self-reflection. Taking a few minutes a day to meditate, breathe deeply, and tune in to our own energy can make a big difference in our connection to the cosmos.

Nature also plays a fundamental role in our cosmic connection. We often find ourselves trapped inside buildings and surrounded by technology, which can take us away from the beauty and serenity that Mother Nature affords us. Try to spend time outdoors, whether it's taking a walk in the woods, sitting in a park, or simply enjoying the sun in your garden. Observe the cycles of life around you and let them inspire you to connect with the universe on a deeper level.

In addition, it's important to pay attention to our energy and how we interact with the world around us. We are always exchanging energy with the people, places and situations we encounter throughout the day. Being aware of our interactions and ensuring that we maintain a positive and respectful attitude with all the beings we encounter allows us to maintain a constant energy balance.

A practical way to integrate cosmic connection into our daily lives is through the practice of gratitude. Often, we focus on what we lack or on the challenges we face, forgetting to appreciate what we already have. Cultivating an attitude of gratitude allows us to value the gifts of the universe and to recognize the blessings that come our way every day. From the simple act of giving thanks for a new dawn to expressing gratitude to the significant people and experiences in our lives, gratitude helps us to open up to the cosmic connection of abundance and love.

We cannot underestimate the power of our intentions in integrating cosmic connection into our daily lives. Our intentions are like seeds that we plant in the universe, and through them, we manifest our reality. Each day, take a moment to set a clear, positive intention for your journey. Visualize how you want your day to unfold, what energies you want to attract and what you want to achieve. Then, keep that intention present throughout the day, reminding yourself that you are connected to the cosmos and that you have the power to create a reality full of harmony and well-being.

As we begin to integrate these practical tips into our lives, we open up to a new dimension of cosmic connection and energy balance. However, this is only the beginning of our journey. In the second half of this chapter, we will explore additional techniques that will allow us to deepen our connection and live in tune with the interconnected universe. Stay tuned to discover new ways to nourish your cosmic connection and expand your energy balance in the next installment!

Remember, boldly and curiously engage in this exploration of cosmic connection in your daily life. The universe is waiting to guide you on your path to wholeness and connection with all beings in the cosmos. Our journey of integrating cosmic connection into our daily lives continues, immersing us even deeper into the depths of our being and into the wonder of the interconnected universe that surrounds us. In this second half of this chapter, we will dive into additional techniques that will allow us to deepen our connection and live in tune with energy balance.

As we explore the possibilities of nourishing our cosmic connection, it's essential to remember to practice self-acceptance and self-care. The cosmic connection is about understanding that we are an integral part of this vast universe and that we deserve to love and care for ourselves as much as we do for others. Spend time doing things that make you feel good, whether it's enjoying a relaxing bath, reading an inspiring book, or spending quality time with yourself. Take every opportunity to reconnect with yourself and recognize that you deserve love and attention just as much as any other being in the cosmos.

Another powerful technique that we can use to integrate cosmic connection into our daily lives is creative visualization. Visualization is a powerful tool that allows us to use our imaginations to create a clear and vibrant mental image of what we want to manifest in our lives. Take a few minutes each day to close your eyes and visualize your deepest dreams and desires. As you immerse yourself in this visualization, imagine how it feels, what it looks like, and how your ideal reality unfolds. Allow cosmic energy to flow through you and fill your visualizations with bright and powerful light. Creative visualization is a bridge to the manifestation of our deepest desires and helps us to align with the flow of the universe.

In addition, it's important to remember that we are part of an interconnected community of human beings and other living beings. Our cosmic connection invites us to treat others with compassion and empathy, recognizing that we all share the same cosmic origin and destiny. Look for opportunities to help others and practice acts of love and kindness. Even the smallest gestures, such as a smile or a kind word, can have a positive impact on another person's life and strengthen our connection to the cosmos.

To further deepen our cosmic connection, we can explore spiritual practices and philosophies that invite us to expand our awareness and understanding of the universe. Whether through meditation, prayer, reading sacred texts, or participating in ancient rituals, each of us can find a spiritual discipline that resonates with our own quest for cosmic connection. These practices will help us to broaden our perspective and to live in harmony with the universal flow of energy.

As we integrate these new knowledge and practices into our daily lives, we realize that the cosmic connection is not just something that makes us feel good, but a way of living in coherence with our true essence. Through constant practice, our lives are transformed into a harmonious dance with the universe, where our intentions and actions align with a greater purpose.

As this second half of the chapter comes to an end, I invite you to continue exploring and experimenting with the teachings shared here. Don't stop here, continue your journey of cosmic connection, opening yourself up to new possibilities and to the wisdom of the universe.

Always remember that you are part of something bigger and that your cosmic connection will guide you every step of the way. Keep your hearts open and curious, and remember that the universe is always present, waiting to support you in your quest for wholeness and well-being.

May the cosmic connection illuminate your path and bless you every moment of your existence.

Namaste.

Disclaimer

The information provided in this book is for general informational and educational purposes only. The author and publisher make no representation or warranties with respect to the accuracy, applicability, fitness, or completeness of the contents of this book. They are not intended to be a substitute for professional advice, diagnosis, or treatment. The author and publisher shall not be held liable for any loss or damage allegedly arising from any information or suggestions within this book.

By reading this book, you agree that you are solely responsible for your own decisions and actions. If you require specific advice for your personal situation, consult with a qualified professional.

The views expressed by the author do not necessarily reflect the views of the publisher. All information is provided on an as-is basis.

Don't miss out!

Visit the website below and you can sign up to receive emails whenever Gonzalo Estrada publishes a new book. There's no charge and no obligation.

https://books2read.com/r/B-A-OZBBB-AHEZC

BOOKS2READ

Connecting independent readers to independent writers.

Also by Gonzalo Estrada

Self Healing
Visualiza tu Éxito
Cultivando Líderes
Afirmaciones y Empoderamiento
Semillas de Cambio
Cómo convertir TikTok en una máquina de hacer dinero
Cómo hacer dinero con Pinterest
Cómo hacer un ensayo
Cómo Pedir un Aumento de Sueldo
Currículo Poderoso
Entrenamiento sin Violencia
Entrevista Laboral
Gana Dinero con X (Twitter)
Ganar Masa Muscular
Volver a Empezar; el arte de reinventarse
Analiza Resuelve Ejecuta
Aromatherapy, The natural path to your pet´s well being
Holistic Feeding
The ABC of Educating Your Pet
The Art of Cosmic Connection
The Art of Feng Shui applied to your Pets

9 798224 133727